IN THE
NATIONAL INTEREST

General Sir John Monash once exhorted a graduating class to 'equip yourself for life, not solely for your own benefit but for the benefit of the whole community'. At the university established in his name, we repeat this statement to our own graduating classes, to acknowledge how important it is that common or public good flows from education.

Universities spread and build on the knowledge they acquire through scholarship in many ways, well beyond the transmission of this learning through education. It is a necessary part of a university's role to debate its findings, not only with other researchers and scholars, but also with the broader community in which it resides.

Publishing for the benefit of society is an important part of a university's commitment to free intellectual inquiry. A university provides civil space for such inquiry by its scholars, as well as for investigations by public intellectuals and expert practitioners.

This series, In the National Interest, embodies Monash University's mission to extend knowledge and encourage informed debate about matters of great significance to Australia's future.

Professor Margaret Gardner AC
President and Vice-Chancellor,
Monash University

LOUISE NEWMAN

RAPE CULTURE

MONASH
UNIVERSITY
PUBLISHING

Monash University Publishing
Matheson Library Annexe
40 Exhibition Walk
Monash University
Clayton, Victoria 3800, Australia
https://publishing.monash.edu

Monash University Publishing brings to the world publications which advance the best traditions of humane and enlightened thought.

ISBN: 9781922464651 (paperback)
ISBN: 9781922464668 (ebook)

Series: In the National Interest
Editor: Louise Adler
Project manager & copyeditor: Paul Smitz
Designer: Peter Long
Typesetter: Cannon Typesetting
Proofreader: Gillian Armitage
Printed in Australia by Ligare Book Printers

A catalogue record for this book is available from the National Library of Australia.

PREFACE

In June 2021, the Federal Court released a transcript of an interview conducted by the ABC's Louise Milligan a year earlier with Jo Dyer.[1] The interview concerned Dyer's long-time friend Kate, who in February 2020 had accused attorney-general Christian Porter of raping her when she was sixteen, and it formed part of the evidence in the case of Christian Porter versus the Australian Broadcasting Commission. The interviewer and interviewee are cogent, methodical and ethical individuals, each playing their role with integrity and the appropriate gravitas.

There are two particularly striking features of the account of Kate's encounter with Christian Porter at the University of Sydney in 1988 and its after-effects.

The first is that Kate is routinely described by those who knew her as a highly skilled debater: according to her friends, speaking—in particular public speaking—'meant an enormous amount to her'. The second is that her story has only ever been told publicly by friends, lawyers and journalists, with the latter variously prurient, politically motivated, personally invested or committed to the 'public interest' principle. Kate herself never had a chance to speak. She killed herself a day after withdrawing the complaint she had made to police only months earlier. In this tragic story, speech begets violence, despair and death—as in so many other stories of rape and abuse, speech and violence go hand in hand.

Psychoanalysis is about precisely these issues— what it is possible to say and the deadly effects of denial and invalidation. Indeed, it might be uniquely suited to an age in which speaking—who can speak, who has the right to speak, and for whom—are abiding cultural preoccupations. The fact that psychoanalysis has been marginalised, in favour of psychological remedies that privilege the banishment of symptoms, says a great deal about the hypocrisies of our moment. And what is our moment? I believe we are living in a 'rape culture', where the abuse of women is normalised, seen as inevitable, acceptable, untreatable.

RAPE CULTURE

Recent revelations of sexual harassment, abuse and assault in the Australian Parliament have prompted a range of responses. Political leaders have attempted to limit the damage by referring to the lack of criminal charges, and they have resisted discussion of the seemingly embedded nature of misogyny. Advocates for survivors see this as the continuation of a long history of the cultural normalisation of the abuse of women and an attempt to perpetuate abuse through legal mechanisms and the exercise of power. The government's response has been a series of anxious manoeuvres designed to obfuscate, delay and stonewall using so-called inquiries and clichés about respect for women. Some of the media coverage also has been of concern, with crude and ill-informed discussion of individual allegations with an apparent lack of awareness of the impact of trauma on victims.

At the same time, young women survivors are acknowledging the reality of abuse and demanding reforms. Young women in schools are speaking out about the institutionalised abuse of girls and the impact this is having on their development and mental health. Within Australia's history is the systematic abuse of colonised Indigenous women, but abuse is not solely an issue of ethnicity, race, class or location. Women of all social backgrounds, ages and occupations are being assaulted and abused, and far too few are able to access support and speak about their experiences. The silence around the deeply entrenched cultural conditions that permit misogyny is deafening.

We might have expected the political leadership of the day to respond to this outpouring of evidence. But we are still waiting. And while we wait, women continue to suffer violence.

Saxon Mullins, who alleged she was raped in a laneway behind a Kings Cross club in 2013 and spent four years unsuccessfully pursuing the case; Brittany Higgins, a former political staffer who alleges that she was raped by a colleague in a ministerial office in Parliament House in 2019; Chanel Contos, whose online petition demanding earlier and better sex education in schools prompted over 6000 testimonies of abuse from former Sydney schoolgirls; 2021 Australian of the Year Grace Tame, who was repeatedly sexually abused by a teacher when she was fifteen; Kate— these are just some of the women whose horrific stories of abuse have become public knowledge in recent times. And yet, although there have been reputational consequences for the men who have been 'outed' as abusers, nothing has really changed.

The gender wars continue unabated, with women's bodies and minds both the object of dispute and the prize for those with power. The misogyny that structures and shapes women's daily lives has become part of Australia's collective cultural mythology—timeless and universal, a given that is beyond debate, an immutable fact of the relationship between men and women. Of course, there is nothing irrevocable about misogyny, but it has been a reality for women for so long, and a mode of conduct for men for so long, that it has become 'Just the way things are …' So women are supposed to dress modestly, stay home, stay sober, so as not to provoke the latent and apparently natural desire of men to hurt or kill them.

Yes, there is much work to be done to understand why misogyny exists, to determine what prompts men's rage and hostility towards women and how they might be helped, possibly cured. But in this book, my focus is on the impact of rape culture on its victims, especially how women respond to the experience of living in a rape culture, and what happens to our minds and bodies within it.

The current wave of protests is an attempt to speak out, to break away from the paralysis of shame and fear that protects perpetrators and the systems that shield them. Survivors of abuse are hoping to create a shift towards the acknowledgement of their experiences, a shift that will allow them to hold the perpetrators of abuse to account. The disclosures have their genesis in the Me Too movement, which has triggered an outpouring of truth-telling. And while the issue of identity continues to animate and agitate conservative commentators, identity politics has enabled a more nuanced attitude towards our sense of self. Call it 'challenging gender categories' if you will, but the prospect of blurring the distinctions between masculinity and femininity is surely a welcome advance. It is in this sociocultural arena of shifting representations that new narratives may emerge, as opposed to short-term political slogans. However, we are nonetheless left with the question of whether it is possible to use this moment to promote cultural change when the processes of power work for the protection of the powerful and offer only tokenistic rhetorical homilies.

While we may be living in an era of large social movements—climate change, Occupy Wall Street, Black Lives Matter, Me Too—we have been here before. Those of us who lived through the social revolution of the 1970s, and in particular the women's movement with its emphasis on the personal as political, look at the current struggles with both hope and concern. The powerful voices of a younger generation give us optimism, but the issues confronting them remain so sadly familiar. We thought we had changed the world forever, that sexism and misogyny had become the last refuge of the few remaining troglodytes. But we were wrong. It is time to think again about why and how this seemingly immutable system of power and control persists.

Breaking the silence is an important part of dismantling and challenging power. But there is a heavy price to be paid by the women who speak truth to power, be it in politics, academia, at home or in the workplace. That cost is both personal and professional and it includes vilification, the loss of jobs, reputational damage and long-term psychological impacts. The women who stood outside Parliament House in March 2021 for March 4 Justice and declared 'Enough is enough!' were signalling their own lived experiences, their rage, their resistance. Telling personal stories to bring about change is a powerful act, but it's also painful as individual women become targets. The trauma of the abuse is compounded by the trauma of the retelling and the awful realisation that this is dangerous. These truth-tellers know that in speaking out, they risk their credibility and their safety.

Historically, women survivors have been portrayed as mentally unwell, hysterical, delusional, as vindictive liars. Apparently, women's bodies and minds contribute heavily to this state of instability and lack of competence—women are ruled by their hormones, they are hypersexual or frigid, they are unable to regulate their emotions or relationships, or they are controlling. Contradictions abound, but coherence or consistency has never mattered in a rape culture that portrays women as unreliable historians while their perpetrators are believed and supported as they defeat 'false allegations'.

In a succession of court cases, we also have seen the theory of 'false memories' deployed to undermine women's testimonies, to question the reliability of traumatic childhood events recollected in adulthood. It often can take more than twenty or thirty years for survivors to disclose their abuse, so they become easy targets for combative defence lawyers. Survivors' memories and recollections of trauma are deemed erroneous, implanted by biased and overenthusiastic campaigning therapists. Indeed, false memory is routinely used as a legal defence, although there are very few therapists who encourage this form of treatment, which urges women to remember details of abuse that has been only partly recalled. The reality is that most trauma is recalled, not forgotten—even when the forgetting would be a small mercy for the survivor. Memories almost inevitably return and are 'spoken' in different ways, including through bodily experience, in nightmares and via a range of anxieties. These manifestations are not easily understood or accommodated within the legal system, with its demands for a simplistic narrative.

Trauma shapes the capacity to recall and make sense of overwhelming experiences, as well as the process of speaking out. It is pervasive and frightening for survivors, who need to create a narrative and find meaning in their suffering. The public discussion of trauma by journalists, politicians and lawyers in the absence of any clinical understanding has been very damaging for truth-telling in the context of allegations. The current system erects barriers against the airing of powerful personal accounts and subsequently their validation.

That is why the Royal Commission into Institutional Responses to Child Sexual Abuse, which delivered its final report in December 2017,[2] was so important. The royal commission heard compelling narratives, given many years after the events in question, and provided evidence of the long-term impact of early trauma and the need for systemic change and therapeutic support. The inquiry provided a space in which women could speak and be validated, offering the prospect of recovery. Yet it also prompted the realisation that processes of accountability and redress are complex and slow.

The current impasse is shaped by deeply held but unacknowledged assumptions; distorted representations of gender, power and the meaning of transgression; and resistance to these norms. It is dangerous for women to speak out because they risk being demonised, diminished or ignored—a 'good woman' is a quiet woman. Speaking out about abuse and rape remains controversial even though we witness the murder of one woman every week in Australia, and unknown cases of rape. This is the unpalatable truth of the deeply embedded and systemic sexual aggression in this country. The past 200 years of our history have been a saga of misogyny that has impacted on women of all colours and classes. That past is now re-enacted in the present, so acknowledging those traumas will influence the future by shifting frameworks of meaning and understanding. The voices of women, clearly heard, are vital for this process to work.

This book is intended to provide a way of thinking about men's need to define, control and regulate women's minds and bodies, as well as the growing opposition to male power and privilege. In my professional work, I see many women survivors of child and adult abuse. The impact of that abuse can be severe, long-lasting and overwhelming. We have various diagnoses for these experiences, which are referred to as complex post–traumatic conditions and are being seen in increasing numbers of women. A crucial element of recovery is building the capacity to speak the truth of experiences—to piece together a greater understanding of trauma that is otherwise too painful to think about. This may include reassembling memories and being able to bear the thought that others are indeed capable of causing great damage.

The stories included here, of some of the women I have worked with, illustrate the struggle to regain a voice and a sense of agency.[3] This reclaiming of one's voice is precisely what is denied women in their interactions with the legal system, and in other situations where women's accounts are routinely undermined.

UNDERSTANDING WHAT WOMEN WANT

Over the past few years in particular, women have been giving voice to their distress and anger about sexual harassment, discrimination and denigration. The stories of violence towards women and children are now so graphically recounted and so common-place that they have become a sort of pornography of male hatred. In their wake have come calls for women to restrict their activities, change their dress codes and stay at home as a form of sexual quarantine, but with little corresponding discussion of male behaviour. A profound hatred of women is normalised and accepted as part of the natural order of things. What will it mean to change this entrenched cultural system? Do those in power who benefit from this rape culture have the capacity to acknowledge it?

The overarching aims of rape culture are to maintain traditional gender and power structures and to reinforce the excluded and disempowered role of women and minority groups. The means to do this are now embedded in political and legal processes and are effectively used to minimise and distort the reality of abuse, and to blame women. This is evidenced by the low rates of reporting of abuse and rape, the low rates of conviction, and the endless inquiries following incidents with little translation into change.

So far, the political responses to protests and calls for broad social reform can be character-ised as inept attempts to control and minimise debate. Political leaders exert tight control of the narrative, focused as they are on that day's news cycle. When thousands of women marched on Parliament House for March 4 Justice, neither Prime Minister Scott Morrison nor Minister for Women Marise Payne determined it was in their or anyone else's interests to address the protest. Instead, the PM announced an inquiry into workplace safety and complaints processes, a poorly disguised way of not investigating allegations of sexual assault. And so, while primitive displays of sexual behaviour are blandly condemned, there has been no analysis of why a workplace like Parliament House, apparently Australia's 'seat of democracy', continues to consider the denigration of women and the assertion of male privilege normal and acceptable professional conduct. There has been no calling to account, no analysis, no apology, leaving only the most optimistic of individuals to see the possibility of change. The notion, embraced by political leaders, that the sudden appointment of several women to the Coalition Cabinet—including the anti–abortion rights Assistant Minister for Women Amanda Stoker[4]—would be a panacea, tells us that women's rights are undervalued and under threat.

Women, of course, are often seen as incapable of 'knowing' their own minds. Hence, they need male guidance and control; they are seen as feeble and childlike, forever overreacting to perceived abuse and mistreatment. When women do find a voice and name their attackers, the immediate response is disbelief and the invention of counter-narratives of seductive and manipulative women who invited, provoked or fabricated abuse.

Sigmund Freud once said, 'The great question that has never been answered, and which I have not yet been able to answer, despite my thirty years of research into the feminine soul, is "What does a woman want?"' To be heard, to be respected and to live in safety would be a good starting point.

DISPUTED TERRITORY

Fundamental to rape culture is the disputed territory of the female body. Women's bodies are the targets of regulation, control and attack, just as they are sources of shame and humiliation. Brittany Higgins and her alleged rapist were admitted around two o'clock on a Saturday morning into then defence minister Linda Reynolds's office in Parliament House, despite the fact that Higgins was clearly heavily inebriated—none of the security guards inquired about her welfare because she had clearance to be in the office, not even when she was later found alone in the office, lying naked on a couch, asleep. In what universe is it acceptable for an unconscious and abandoned naked young woman to be left unattended and uncared for? Are security guards so inured to appalling conduct in 'The People's House' that they didn't feel the need to make sure Higgins was feeling OK, and at least cover her with a blanket to help ensure her privacy?

Battles over women's bodies are really battles over female identity, begging questions such as whether men and women experience their bodies in the same way, and whether being a woman is a biologically determined experience. It is no accident that, despite living in the twenty-first century, we are once again witnessing attacks on women's reproductive rights and access to abortion that mostly had been in remission since the early 1970s, at least in the West. In some parts of the United States, for example, the lack of access to contraception and termination has made reproduction compulsory, thereby bypassing any notion of autonomy and consent. Gilead in the real world.

Arguments over the relationship between women and their bodies have long centred on the relationship between biology/nature and reason. Such dualisms underlie traditional Western conceptions of masculinity and femininity. Historically, women have been defined as closer to nature and ruled by biology, humours, hormones or their troublesome uteruses. They have been described as less rational subjects, unable to attain full subjectivity like the transcendent male; they have been perceived as having a flawed moral conscience and being intrinsically more prone to the effects of uncontained sexual desires than men. The 'cures' for female ailments, particularly in the Victorian era, have included sexual massage by male physicians, clitoridectomies and physical containment, as ways of getting rid of troubling feelings. The female body—particularly the unwell female body of the so-called hysteric—also was a major focus of attention in early theatrical performances, with highly sexualised spasmodic states and eager male audiences.

Of course, we can fast forward to our own moment in history and consider, however distasteful it is, the case of former film producer Harvey Weinstein and his casting couch. Weinstein's seemingly inexhaustible sexual appetites depended on a succession of disenfranchised actors to fulfil his needs. Greater than a desire for sex, perhaps, is the predator's need to exercise power. The female actor in search of work, in search of an opportunity to be made visible on-screen, first had to become the object of Weinstein's gaze—she was forced to accede to his power if she was to be seen. Because if she is not seen, then who is she? An actor's entire identity is formed around being watched, so they would make their bodies perform for Weinstein and then, if they were lucky, for a mass audience of cinemagoers. Weinstein rendered visible over 100 women who later came forward to accuse him of sexual harassment. That was his power and these women's powerlessness.

Since Simone de Beauvoir's revolutionary 1949 book *The Second Sex*, there has been plenty of discussion about the significance of women's experiences of their bodies: menstruation, birth and sexual experiences, and how these are incorporated, or not, into feminine identity. De Beauvoir distinguishes between sex as biological and gender as a social construct. She writes that the experience of girls and women is of the body as the object of the other's gaze; this scrutiny is internalised and becomes an intense self-monitoring of desirability and horror with the onset of puberty and menstruation. We see this in descriptions from women experiencing anorexia: their battle for control of the body, the need to take up no space and remain eternally infantile in bodily form.

De Beauvoir also describes the pregnant state as one of being 'plant and animal … an incubator and life's passive instrument'.[5] Contemporary feminists have rejected this proposition as we make sense of the ambivalence directed at the maternal body, stressing the value inherent in this nurturing state and the positive power of the reproductive body. The female body, in all its messiness, its fluids, its fecundity, its interiority, is what men fear and want to repel, but also to dominate and control.

MODERN HYSTERIA

Hysteria has long been a convenient label for describing the woman who resists control, the woman who won't be silenced, the woman who demands to be heard. Hysteria has a central role in rape culture because it is an easy way of pathologising women, but it also tells powerful stories of the reality of abuse. This is why reclaiming the notion of hysteria as a form of communication and protest has been a significant project for the feminists re-examining Freud.

The concept of modern hysteria, and the changing form and understanding of the hysterical condition, are discussed by Juliet Mitchell in *Mad Men and Medusas*.[6] She argues that hysteria is a response to dilemmas concerning emotional identity, and that our social context shapes both the symptoms and our understanding of the mind in conflict. Modern hysteria has various expressions, including pain, eating disorders, borderline states and manifestations of dissociation. Mitchell writes that hysteria's many manifestations have shown some striking similarities throughout the ages: sensations of suffocation, choking, breathing and eating difficulties, mimetic imitations, shocks and seizures, states of withdrawal, sexual desire. Treatments have ranged from encouraging display to punishment.

When hysteria disappears, we need to ask: where did it go? The answer is that its absence is only temporary, that it eventually emerges in other ways—as conflict, the repression of desire, as a taboo on expression. In fact, so-called borderline personality disorders stemming from early sexual abuse have become the contemporary version of hysteria. Early abusive experiences can disrupt interpersonal relatedness, the capacity to function psychologically, and our defences—against knowing about trauma and betrayal, and against unacknowledged feelings. Importantly, current diagnostic terminology can also be used to control and denigrate survivors.

Even the definitions used in clinical practice to describe bodily dysfunction reflect the mystery of the female body as a model of fragility and mental instability. For example, 'chronic pelvic pain of unknown aetiology' is a condition in which women live with severe pain that impacts their functioning, and which can be associated with depression and distress. Cures on offer include nerve blocks, vaginal dilatations and neuroleptics (antipsychotics). But with increasing awareness of child abuse contributing to an increasing number of reports to child protection agencies, why wouldn't a clinician pause to consider the origins of that pain, to ask whether the body in question might be expressing a traumatic history?

Women may present to mental health services with a range of issues, including dissociative episodes, self-harm, multiple somatic complaints, poor affective regulation, and significant disruption to psychological cohesion. Kindly mental health professionals will make a note of 'complex trauma disorder in child abuse survivors'. But increasingly we are seeing the presentation of dissociative identity symptoms in which early trauma is acknowledged but also elaborated into pseudo-explanatory narratives of satanic rituals, organised paedophilia and alien abductions, which are more easily disbelieved and dismissed. While these presentations can easily be seen as trauma-related, social and cultural factors clearly are also shaping the trauma narratives.

Social withdrawal, a refusal to eat or drink, a lack of response to pain, and comatose states are designated part of a 'conversion disorder/pervasive refusal syndrome'. This is seen in children and adolescents in situations of inescapable familial trauma, and in severely entrapped and traumatised groups such as asylum seekers. It is a response of helplessness and devitalisation in the face of unresolvable dilemmas. Chronic fatigue syndrome and the current proliferation of chemical and food sensitivities are other symptoms of social and psychological problems—they are a response to a disordered world in which one is powerless. What is common to these states is a profound lack of the capacity to speak, to put words to traumatic concerns. Limited reflective capacity and reductive pseudo-medical explanations offer a narrative of disease, a role, and engagement with a system of care and science. What is left unresolved and uncared for is the body in question, the trauma it expresses, and the culture that produced it.

Pregnancy brings its own dilemmas, such as expectations around the experience of gestation and birth, and the desire for autonomy and self-regulation. The pregnant woman may yearn for a profound sense of fusion with her baby as a perfect, yet also a competing, relationship. However, women are often deeply ambivalent about fertility control and multiple terminations—they can deny the changes in their bodies and resist making meaning out of their condition. We see instances of neonaticide and infanticide in relation to traumatic conception (rape), earlier abuse and dissociation. The pregnant body, ostensibly a sign of optimism about the future, in the traumatised woman can be a devastating reminder of her own suffering, doubt and loss of agency.

THE BODY TELLS THE STORY: OPHELIA

The male gaze is a harsh judge, and attempts to garner its approval can be devastating for some women. But bodies can also be sources of resistance.

Ophelia was sixteen years old when I saw her over several months as an inpatient in a mental health unit. Her story allows us to reflect on contemporary notions of the body, trauma and hysteria. This case could be named 'A Modern Dora', after one of Freud's most famous patients, whom I will discuss later in this book. But Ophelia's story actually captures the presentation of a young woman, largely inaccessible in her fugue, her deeply regressed state, who used her body in a powerful way to tell an unspeakable tale. For Ophelia, this disguised telling—letting her body say what she couldn't verbalise—raised the real risk of death when the body had done enough truth-telling.

When I first met Ophelia she was mute and made no eye contact, instead hiding her face behind long straggly hair. Pale and thin, she had a nasogastric tube, having had no oral intake for eight months, not even water. She held onto a plastic bag into which she repeatedly spat in a disgusted way. When sitting, she writhed and contorted her body and limbs, sometimes making sounds of pain, and she screamed and lashed out if touched. She wore a long white gown and was strikingly similar in appearance to the early depictions of hysterics. The hospital staff described Ophelia as often silent, bed-bound for long periods, and incontinent. On the occasions when she did speak, she shouted obscenities at the staff, sometimes removing her clothes and spreading her legs. She also had episodes of frenzied aggression, kicking and hitting staff and her mother, who was a frequent visitor.

Ophelia resisted any attempts to offer her food and would forcibly kick the meal away. She was on a 'desensitisation' program of food exposure, to which she reacted very negatively. She needed sedation to change her nasogastric tube and often pulled it out; she even attempted to strangle herself with the tubing, sometimes with her bedsheets, although in an ineffectual way. She often appeared dazed, unresponsive to the environment, and she would 'pass out' following particularly disturbed periods.

Ophelia aroused huge anxiety in the staff of the mental health unit. She was seen as a major puzzle, subjected to extensive investigations, and there was also a very real risk in terms of her nutritional status and suicidality. Ophelia's mother described her as having been a sickly child, with a long history of health issues and numerous medical reviews. However, despite this, Ophelia was said to have been bright and formerly socially engaged, maintaining good relationships with her two older siblings throughout early primary school. The mother denied any family conflicts and focused instead on possible biological explanations for Ophelia's state of mute withdrawal, convinced her daughter's condition was due to some sort of viral or immune system disorder.

On the one occasion when she was visited by her father, Ophelia shouted that he had sexually abused her and tried to hit him. Child protection authorities became involved, but Ophelia then lapsed into an unconscious state for several weeks.

From a psychological perspective, the questions that need to be asked here do not concern truth or falsity but rather what Ophelia was communicating, verbally and otherwise. What was Ophelia saying through her body, and was it possible for her to escape this? When Ophelia did speak, this was followed by deep withdrawal, as if the words had damaged her and should not have been uttered. She had no language to describe her experiences and seemed trapped in her body. It is a situation that is ongoing—at the time of writing, Ophelia is still in hospital, deeply regressed.

In a rape culture, what a woman can control is her body, as a response to abuse, to the feelings of powerlessness that follow. Desperate acts such as starving and gorging are attempts to control what seems uncontrollable when one is buffeted by the needs and demands of others. The body, which is inescapably associated with social value, self-esteem and identity, becomes the last bastion of a sense of self and agency. The refusal to conform to social expectations increasingly takes the form of anorexia (think of the pro-ana movement, which bestows approval on self-starvation and a skeletal image) or the other extreme of morbid obesity. The struggle for control of the body is a proxy for the struggle for selfhood: is this body mine? Who is in charge of my body? Controlling what is taken into the body and what is expelled from it feels like power to the powerless.

It isn't difficult to see the connections here with sexual autonomy and the need for safety. As a consequence, an ambivalent and frequently toxic engagement with the medical system becomes an epic battle, often one without resolution. The focus on how the body looks is simultaneously a defence against the conflicts around gendered identity, an expression of resistance, and an attempt to shape the fundamental elements of autonomy, safety and attachment. Nothing can be spoken, so the body itself becomes a form of language. It also becomes the preoccupation, leaving no energy or capacity to reflect on the powerful, ironically all-consuming feelings of hunger, emptiness and fullness, pleasure and frustration.

Roxane Gay, in *Hunger: A Memoir of (My) Body*, describes eating after being sexually assaulted by a gang at the age of twelve:

> I am hollowed out. I was determined to fill the void and food was what I used to build a shield around what little was left of me. I ate and ate and ate in the hope that if I made myself huge my body would be safe.[7]

In recent public appearances, Gay has spoken about her desire to take up space, her refusal to be small or invisible, but also her lack of agency. Gay's desire for visibility and legitimacy are fundamental dilemmas of female identity. The embodied self is not actually independent or self-defined; instead, it is defined by the (male) gaze it attracts or repels, the moral judgements it engenders, and the attempts made to regulate that body's appearance and existence. The fat female body becomes the site of a battle for autonomy, and so it is a stark representation of the impulse to resist.

When, in May 2017, Mia Freedman, founder of the media company Mamamia, sought to interview Roxanne Gay for a podcast, she mused about whether the author would fit in the lift of her Sydney office, and whether she had a chair that would fit Gay's 200-kilo frame.[8] Were these reasonably expressed and appropriate concerns, or a moment of fat shaming and an act of judgemental disrespect? For Gay, who is black, it was a humiliating 'shit show' in which a thin, cossetted, rich white woman proved Gay's point: that the female body is a projection of the fears of others and that autonomy for women is all too often a bitter struggle. The morbidly obese or anorexic body can be an act of resistance, of parody, of sexual enactment or fetishism. In both versions of the body, women are revealing either a sense of power or subjugation. At stake is a woman's desire for autonomy and the lack of it.

THE ACCEPTANCE OF SUFFERING:
ELIZABETH

Elizabeth was a 32-year-old woman who lived with a female friend and worked part-time as a graphic designer. She initially came to me seeking support for her eating disorder, depression and high-risk sexual behaviour. At 180 kilograms, she was classed as morbidly obese. She had recently had investigations for possible polycystic ovarian syndrome, having experienced menstrual irregularity. When a gynae-endocrinologist recommended gastric banding, she became extremely angry and expressed a powerful desire to self-harm.

I first met Elizabeth in the waiting area outside my office, where she was standing due to the size of the available chair. It was a hot day and she was dressed in a very short silk slip dress in bright pink, which was striking against her olive skin. Her hair was long and unkempt. She moved with difficulty, being somewhat breathless, and eventually sat on my office sofa. She appeared amorphous, mountainous, but with a very young-looking, attractive face.

Her clothing allowed a ritualistic display of flesh, simultaneously sexual and maternal, rather like the Venus de Milo. Initially smiling, she said she was not sure why she'd come, as she didn't really want anything other than to stop bingeing and vomiting.

Elizabeth was an only child who was estranged from her parents. Her mother had separated from her father when Elizabeth was three years of age and remarried three years later. Elizabeth described her mother as cold, punishing and physically abusive. She never had a sense that her mother was protective or available, and spoke of her in derogatory terms. Her early memories of her father were idealised—she'd felt a profound sense of grief when he left and blamed her mother. Elizabeth said she had been getting bigger and bigger since around seven years of age, when she was abused by her new stepfather. Her mother had ridiculed her for her weight gain, telling her she would never be attractive to men. This made her comply with her stepfather's sexual overtures—she recalled thinking, 'He loves my body'. The abuse continued until she left home at the age of fifteen to live with an aunt, due to the increasing conflict and violence between her mother and stepfather.

During her teenage years, Elizabeth cut herself and suffered episodes of depression. Her weight steadily increased and she was binge eating to the point of severe abdominal pain, vomiting and collapse, which would be followed by exhaustion and sleep. She said this was like the release she now felt after having sex with strangers. She said she wanted to maintain a large and safe body and reacted very negatively when anyone suggested she try and lose weight, or that she would be more attractive if she did. She said she did not want to be attractive in any conventional sense; rather, she had realised that some people desired her as she was now, and she was exploring this.

Elizabeth had a limited social circle and described herself as queer and polymorphous-perverse. She had studied art theory, design and gender studies, including gender fluidity, at a tertiary level and was intelligent and articulate, but she was unresponsive to any exploration of her experience of her body or eating issues. She had

had several years of 'narrative therapy' in her early twenties, which had focused on reconstructing the abuse inflicted by her stepfather. She was haunted by the attraction she still felt for him. She wondered, if she saw him now, whether she would have sex with him, laughed at the thought, then became silent and pensive.

Elizabeth described herself as a 'sex addict', engaging in casual encounters with men she met on the dating site Tinder who wanted sex with a large woman. She said she both loved and loathed this, that she felt desired but also despised, and she could not really bear to think about why she kept repeating this behaviour. She said she would go home afterwards and repeat her pattern of eating, vomiting and then collapsing; if she woke during the night, she would order in vast amounts of takeaway food. On finishing one session with me, Elizabeth said she was on her way to meet a man, having arranged the date so that it would happen as soon as we were done. I had a strong desire to stop her, anxious about the risk and the destructive nature of these encounters. Elizabeth clearly struggled with a sense of emptiness, self-loathing and a loss of control, alongside an intellectual urge to deny this—she resisted reflection other than to admit it was too painful. She was sometimes angry with me, sometimes playful and witty, and she relished recounting her sexual exploits, which were simultaneously bleak and tragic. She also showed me designs she created of vast and boundary-less female shapes.

One day Elizabeth came to see me in a crisis following a violent sexual assault by a Tinder date she had invited to her apartment, despite discussions we had had about the inherent risk in doing so. She said she did not think about safety in these situations and used her usual language of addiction to describe the compulsion she felt, the need to be desired and to feel that she 'existed in her body'. She required hospital treatment and made a police report, but felt ridiculed and a deep sense of shame. This event prompted more-significant depression and self-harm but also a desire to 'give up' her addiction, which she did. However, the psychological price of this 'giving up' was substantial—Elizabeth's disordered eating behaviour increased alongside her preoccupation with her mother and stepfather, especially a deep wish for some unspecified validation from them. I asked her what she wanted from her mother, and we spoke about how she pursued this need even though she knew on some level that it was unlikely to be met. She talked about a sense of yearning for a mother with a soft and warm body, and recounted a dream where her own mother was cold and stiff and had morphed into a figure with a dangerous crocodile face.

Over the next six months, Elizabeth continued her relentless pattern of eating, having sex and struggling with depression. She appeared to want to shock me, to test my capacity to withstand her behaviour, asking me how I felt when she described her life. I told her I had a mixture of responses: anxiety, puzzlement in trying to understand what was driving her and what she wanted from me. She was disappointed that I didn't admit to feeling disgust or judge her in a moral sense. She went on to describe her regular contact with her mother and stepfather and the tragedy of wishing for apology, acceptance, the validation of her suffering, only to receive negative comments about her body and lack of a stable relationship. She felt overwhelmed at family functions, where she would remain silent and not eat, as this would disgust others— she would then go home and binge-eat to the point of pain.

She was emotionally labile and continued to dress in a revealing style and arrange Tinder dates after sessions. She gained more weight; she had dreams that she had reached the size of a mountain that would then erupt like a volcano. She began having more memories of childhood abuse and experienced increasing confusion about her feelings towards her stepfather. She would become angry and tell me I should never have asked her about this and that it needed to be left alone, that I was 'feeding her distress'. I had images during these sessions of being suffocated by her bulk.

Elizabeth's self-presentation reminded me of the model of femininity that is suggested by the Venus of Willendorf, an 11-centimetre statue of a female form from the Palaeolithic era (which began roughly 2.5 million years ago and lasted until 10 000 BCE) that was found in Austria in 1908. It was thought to have been carried by nomadic peoples. Interpretations of the statue have focused on its maternal features, breasts and genitals, and the links to wonderings about fertility and birth. Some archaeologists have suggested its origins lie in a primal matriarchal goddess religion that predates patriarchal forms of social organisation. Certainly for Elizabeth, her relationship with her body evoked a failure of early maternal attachment, entrapment in an abusive dynamic, and a desire to resist that abuse. She described the men she had met in adulthood as 'feeders', likening them to the men in certain reality TV documentaries who feed women to the point of death. Did Elizabeth hope that one of her Tinder dates would put her out of her misery in this way?

Elizabeth used her knowledge of gender theory to justify the maintenance of her weight and her resistance to the 'dieting industry'. She argued that her refusal to conform demonstrated her ability to transcend her current plight—she was determined to survive and control male desire. As she put it, she saw herself as 'bigger than this'. Elizabeth was engaged in an heroic struggle or quest for a safe maternal figure. She fought with both the desire for and disgust with the maternal body. She fashioned her own body as excessive and uncontained, too large and engulfing, which then aroused complex feelings of fascination, horror, moral panic and self-satisfaction.

Elizabeth eventually moved on to a psychologist who specialised in 'fat affirmation'. She said she could not deal with her childhood trauma and had shifted her perspective to see the past as largely irrelevant. She was intent on maintaining a body that could not be subjected to abuse, punishment and fetishisation. However, while she feigned defiance and self-control, she nonetheless felt abject.

According to Julia Kristeva, the abject is a state of breakdown of boundaries that disturbs conventional identity and cultural concepts—it is a breakdown in the distinctions between the self and the other.[9] Experiences that threaten such borders, at the same time reminding us of their fragility, are simultaneously disturbing, disgusting and full of strange pleasures. A potent mix of feelings is aroused by the boundary-less body. Elizabeth's fat form manifests as an out-of-control body that threatens both social conventions and the regularisation of bodily functions. The fat body is attractive and repulsive, a gross presence but also an absence. Through its very existence, the fat body defies the links between the biological body and the social body.

Similarly, the anorexic body arouses both horror and disgust, admiration and desire, concerning the pre-puberty moment. For the starving there is also pride, the ridiculing of contemporary narcissistic culture through exaggeration, and a sense of powerful community and contagion.

The anorexic asks: can I exist without this body? Can I be powerful but take up no space? Can I live on air and defy the limits of biology? The obese body asks: is 'the self' possible if the body is too visible and intrusive? Can I be seen inside all this flesh or am I defined by the horror of the gaze of the judging male? Is it possible to exist without boundaries or distinctions if that is the price of safety?

THE BODY AS BATTLEGROUND

Ophelia and Elizabeth are victims of a rape culture, a culture of misogyny in which women's bodies are the battleground. Both women struggle to form a sense of themselves beyond punishing themselves. Both are trapped in their minds and their bodies.

Ophelia uses her body to communicate the painful truth that her current relationships are untenable as well as to provide a narrative of trauma. Her only other options are to will herself into a death-like regression or to actually die. Symbolically and poignantly, she continues to try and rid herself of her abusive experiences and the intolerable feelings they engender—she literally tries to spit out her trauma. Elizabeth is trapped in a monstrous body that expresses the creation of a place of safety. She cannot move easily or without pain, and she is tormented by an insatiable appetite for both food and sex. She uses her body as a weapon, reducing herself to a fearful and dreadful corporeality where the self, attachment and reflection are elided and she is stuck in an ideology of pseudo-liberation. She flirts with death and non-existence in a real way but resists thinking about her childhood trauma.

In many ways, these cases are tragedies of modern hysteria that ask therapists to refocus our work in the face of unspeakable pain. We offer the 'talking cure' to women whose response to traumatic events is to take revenge in silence, but Elizabeth and Ophelia demand therapeutic relief from conditions that are unspeakable. The work of the therapist, then, is to help these women find their way to a language by which they can reflect on their suffering and resist turning that suffering against the self and body.

Ophelia and Elizabeth's stories are a stark reminder of the sexualised and abusive culture we inhabit. Their illnesses express themselves explicitly in their bodies, through starvation and overeating— either disappearing the body or rendering it huge and insurmountable. How else might a vulnerable and disempowered young woman respond to a hypersexualised and sexist social environment where the female body is consistently judged, abused and diminished?

Women remain an enigma in contemporary psychology. Our experiences are an addendum to many theories, defined only in relationship to the 'norm' of male experience. Women's issues can only be an afterthought when there is a persistent lack of understanding and research about sex differences and sex-specific approaches. The challenge now is how best to carve out a space in which to think about the specificity and difference of women's experience.

THE SOCIAL AND
THE PERSONAL: JANE

Jane was a thirty-year-old single woman completing research into representations of women and fertility in medieval art. She had always been bright, preoccupied with ideas, and had studied art history, philosophy and gender studies. She was socially isolated and described herself as asexual after having had brief encounters with men and women. Jane had previously undergone long-term psychotherapy for issues relating to early trauma, depression and problems in interpersonal relation-ships. She was in a hostile, dependent relationship with her mother—she despised her mother's uncaring, withholding manner, but desperately wanted her love and praise.

Jane presented as an intensely intellectual woman who read extensively, and who had a capacity for focus and was driven to find answers to the psychological issues and dilemmas that claimed her attention. But she experienced pro-found self-doubt about her intellectual ability and career direction, anxiety in teaching situations, and occasionally was overwhelmed with 'dread', causing her to self-harm or drink to excess. When in these states, she would phone her mother, who usually responded in an angry fashion and told Jane to grow up and review her life.

Jane was referred to me by a sexual assault service due to her wish to forget ongoing intrusive memories of sexual abuse in early childhood by her father, which she said was the major focus of her earlier therapy. She resented any attempts to link her issues to her mother, or to her academic focus or her isolation and withdrawal from social relationships. She claimed her last therapist had no idea about mothers or ambivalence but just wanted Jane to fit in with ideas about femininity, which Jane rejected. On the other hand, Jane did not value the sexual assault service's focus on a power and gender analysis, which ascribed all her questions to trauma. She said she found this approach limited and insufficiently focused on her mind and how it worked.

Since our therapy, Jane has continued her trauma-focused treatment and is now working on the issues that are causing her distress, including attempting to deal with her childhood memories. In time, she may better understand the complex relationship she has with her mother and the way in which this has shaped her capacity to interact with and trust others. She remains introspective, albeit aware of her emotional vulnerability, and she continues to avoid broader thinking around gender and the nature of male violence.

The current focus on sexual harassment, domestic violence and sexual abuse, and the accompanying challenges to ideas about gender roles and power differentials, raise existential issues for women in how they acknowledge and deal with trauma. There are many developing issues that psychotherapists need to consider in treating women in the age of Me Too. How are we to encourage reflection on the social while maintaining a focus on the personal and the new uncertainties about gender and its immutability?

Of course, over a century ago, Freud was dealing with many of the same struggles and acknowledged that many questions remained unanswered concerning the dark continent of femininity. If anything, psychoanalysis has continued to struggle with the 'woman question'. If 'one is not born, but rather becomes, a woman', as Simone de Beauvoir argued in *The Second Sex*, then what is the role of the therapist? How is a woman to make sense of her identity? Is it formed in relationship to the male?

Is our identity created in both loving and unloving familial settings? Or can we invent ourselves? And what is the role of therapy as we consider the possibility of changing representations of women and femininity? In other words, we need to ask about the possibility of the reconstruction of autonomy and identity in the face of sociocultural gender norms and power structures, and relate this in useful ways to victim-survivors who are struggling to overcome abuse.

As clinicians, we directly engage with the impact of gender-based violence on women's identity. But it is incumbent upon us also to reflect on the discussions we are having with patients immersed in social struggles as well as individual distress. We need to continue asking ourselves about what is involved in helping women in a time of crisis.

DORA SAYS 'ME TOO'

Concepts of femininity/masculinity have always been problematic within psychoanalysis. Feminism of the 1960s expressed clear hostility towards key concepts of psychoanalysis such as penis envy, seeing that theory as an attempt to support patriarchal notions and social structures and promote biological determinism. This prompted orthodox analysis to reassert the importance of developmental theories—which see different influences in different periods of a child's life—in the face of criticism that Freud, who was a man of his time, incorrectly viewed women as passive, narcissistic, lacking creativity, inadequate and full of shame. Social analysis of the 1970s focused on the social reinforcement of gender stereotypes to dismantle essentialist models of femininity and masculinity. These sociological perspectives influenced psychotherapy and emphasised gender power and self-empowerment, rather than the darker, murky areas of the unconscious, desire, and the ambiguities of sex.

One of the significant issues that Freud and the women he treated faced was that of silence, how to acknowledge and then treat the unspeakable. The famous case of 'Dora'—the name Freud used in his writings; the woman's real name was Ida—has come to symbolise the question of femininity and the gendered unconscious, generating extensive and heated debate. Some critics argue that Freud failed to acknowledge the social and familial context in which Dora developed her hysterical symptoms; they speculate that Freud had difficulty acknowledging Dora's socially unacceptable desires.

In 1900, Phillip Bauer took his eighteen-year-old daughter to Freud for treatment. Freud described Dora as being in 'the first bloom of youth—a girl of intelligence and engaging looks'.[10] Bauer wanted Freud to 'cure' Dora, freeing her to accept the advances of a family friend, Herr K, so that he, Dora's father, could continue to have a relationship with Mrs K. Dora in this exchange was a prized object circulated between men within a social circle. Herr K had been pursuing Dora since she was fourteen; he often took her on walks and occasionally gave her gifts. When Dora told her father that Herr K had made an indecent proposal, Bauer agreed with Herr K that she must have imagined the event.

Dora came to Freud with a range of 'hysterical symptoms', including coughing, difficulty breathing, aphonia (loss of the voice), migraines and lethargy.

She offered him two richly detailed dreams. In the first, Dora's father wakes her up because the house is on fire. Dora wants to leave but her mother is looking for her jewellery case. Dora's father then declares that their lives matter more than his wife's jewellery case. Freud pointed out that 'jewellery case' in the common parlance of the time meant 'vagina'. According to the psychoanalyst, Dora in reality was worried about the danger to her own 'jewellery case', and in her dream her father wants to protect her. Freud believed that Dora was working through her own dangerous desires for Herr K in the dream.

In her second dream, Dora finds a letter from her mother telling her that her father is dead and a funeral is to take place. Dora needs to catch a train to the service but she can't find the station, despite being repeatedly assured that it is nearby. When she finally arrives, she discovers she is too late for the funeral. Freud saw Dora's dream as a fantasy of revenge against her father.

After three months of therapy, Dora abruptly left Freud, who would describe the case as a 'fragment of an analysis'. It is an early example of psychoanalytic dialogue with a focus on both remembering and forgetting, and the expression of repressed symptoms.

Freud's role within the University of Vienna and Dora's father's business activities were both imperilled by the rise of anti-Semitism in the Austrian capital in the 1900s. The unspoken nature of Dora's dangerous desires echoed the unspoken and increasingly dangerous situation for the Viennese Jews. Safety, fear and the nature of the unspoken resonated at the social, familial and psychological levels as Dora described her quest for identity and autonomy within a highly repressive patriarchal system of exchange.

Very real clinical issues also have arisen in the current debates about sexual abuse. Some women experience validation of their concerns, but very few feel supported in the legal processes, and many experience a mixture of shame, guilt, anger and a feeling of being overwhelmed. For some women, identifying as a survivor is empowering and liberating; for others, it may mask ongoing distress and issues of self-blame. Dismantling the paralysing sense of a lack of control and guilt is a key step in recovery and allows for greater understanding of the accountability of perpetrators. Trauma services provide essential initial validation and support to women by helping them rebuild a sense of safety and self-regulation; however, some women may need longer-term mental health interventions, particularly for significant depression and experiences of being 'stuck' with overwhelming emotional distress.

THE PARALYSIS OF
THE SURVIVOR: ANNA

Anna was a 32-year-old single woman on a higher-education research scholarship in science. She had been working part-time on this since moving to Melbourne from interstate four years prior. Anna was referred to me by sexual assault services that had been supporting her through criminal investigations of her abuse at the hands of her father. She was estranged from her mother and siblings, who did not support her legal action—her mother had accused Anna of fabricating stories about her father and dismissed allegations against him involving the abuse of other girls and young women. Anna's father had left the country, but before doing so he'd made frequent attempts to speak with Anna and threatened her. When he was given Anna's address by her mother, Anna had felt betrayed, invalidated and angry.

Anna described being anxious and depressed, and preoccupied with intrusive memories of her father's behaviour throughout her childhood. She recalled being sexually abused from around four years of age until puberty. She said that her father could be nice and playful with her, but then he would touch her in ways she found frightening and confusing—he said she could not tell anyone, as this was their special secret. She grew up, she now understood, with this pathological secret, and she struggled to understand her father's claim that he loved her and that theirs was a positive relationship. She had developed self-loathing and suicidal thoughts.

Throughout the period of abuse, Anna's mother was unavailable and cold. Anna's one attempt to confide in her mother, which she did in a vague way, was rejected. Her mother in fact punished her with isolation if she resisted spending time with her father—her mother slept separately from her father, who would take Anna to his room. Anna felt that her mother must have known what was happening and had handed her over to her father. Meanwhile, Anna's two male siblings were, in her words, very supportive of each other and close to the father, tending at his instigation to tease Anna as being 'too quiet and no fun' and 'weak'. She felt isolated and rejected, with no place in this family.

Anna offered me this account in a flat but fluent monotone that seemed disconnected from her, and with an all-pervasive feeling of sadness and passivity. Her only moment of animation surfaced when recounting her journey with Interpol detectives to find and prosecute her father, and the impact this had on her unsupportive and disbelieving family. She said she had thought about death as far back as she could remember, from around four or five years of age, and that only the prospect of police action had reduced those impulses.

Anna was clearly symptomatic from the point of view of unprocessed trauma. She was required to recount and relive the abuse she suffered, and to inform on her father, whom she alleged had offended against many children. She entertained revenge fantasies where her father died and was haunted by the children he had harmed. She took some comfort in the process of seeking justice, but she also said that while doing so, it was hard to focus on her own recovery, on rebuilding her life. She was withdrawn and had very few social contacts. She had had brief sexual experiences with women over the past few years but found this difficult and did not experience sexual pleasure. She could not tolerate intimacy, nor could she confide in anyone about her family situation or involvement with the police.

Anna described becoming increasingly con-cerned by a range of physical symptoms and multiple inconclusive medical consultations. She felt depressed, was often anxious and panicky, slept poorly and had little appetite. She also was underweight and preoccupied with a loss of muscle and weakness—she would go to the gym and exercise to the point of exhaustion. She wondered if she had a neurological degenerative disorder but then said it was 'probably neurasthenia' (exhaustion due to long-term mental stress or overworking). Anna described abdominal symptoms such as bloating and pain, and placed herself on a gluten-free diet. She experienced migraine-like headaches, episodes of shaking and weakness of the limbs, blurred vision when tired, chronic pelvic pain, and what she felt were hormone-related mood changes. Her GP had recommended several antidepressants, all of which gave her side effects, so she stopped taking them; she was trialled on diazepam when she developed more obvious episodes of panic but also took the medication to help her sleep.

Anna was able to reflect on the impact of the police investigation, but not on her fractured family relationships. She felt that her only 'salvation' and hope for recovery from her abuse and betrayal, which would otherwise haunt her daily, was the quest for justice—even though she was aware that the legal process in no way guaranteed this. She said it felt like she was on a holy mission; as part of the Me Too campaign, she felt she was joining a throng of avengers. The trauma systems of care supported her in this role, but while she found them validating, she sometimes felt that she was not listened to when she spoke about her task. This may partly be because there were clear concerns about her capacity to withstand the perils of her role without descending into chronic invalidism and severe depression. She reminded me of a Joan of Arc figure—with her young, boyish appearance, there was even a physical resemblance.

I felt the need to discuss her lapses into illness, including the meanings of her symptoms, as well as her sense of alienation. Her wish to die was a particular concern, as it seemed to involve a realisation that life and death are fragile and present an ongoing existential dilemma. In talking to me about this, Anna became more agitated, had nightmares about a lack of safety, and subsequently had an episode of preparing for death. She cleaned and organised her house and wrote a final testament, then wandered the streets in a fugue for several hours before being helped home. She felt she was going mad, so frightened was she about having lost all sense of time, and that giving into this might provide an escape.

I was acutely aware of Anna's simplistic but powerful wish that legal action would resolve her traumatic experience, so I was anxious that communicating any doubts about this, about the potential costs of her search for justice, would remove some of the hope she still had. I also thought of psychoanalyst Donald Winnicott's reflection that the catastrophe you fear will happen has already happened earlier in your life—the fear of madness a patient experiences might be an indication that the worst has already happened; it has just been buried or forgotten. Anna was haunted by the legacy of that early betrayal by her parents, and that break-down of attachment was now being reflected in the breakdown of her bodily experience and a more obvious sense of fragmentation and dissociation. Anna's was a complex response to complex trauma.

Like most survivors, Anna had unbearable, traumatic memories of her abuse. These were not 'repressed' as such but were often too painful to dwell on. Her anxiety, her feelings of abandonment and chronic isolation, her real need to better understand her maltreatment—this constellation of effects is common in the severely abused and dramatically impacts their ability to tell their stories, to live with the horror of abuse, and to engage with legal and police processes. The fear of being stuck in the reliving of the experience can be paralysing.

Despite this, women victim-survivors continue to endure attempts to discredit them and to imply that they are mentally ill or unreliable witnesses. Severe trauma affects a survivor's ability to remember and shapes her narrative as she works to communicate the truth of her experience and to protect herself. What our clinical assessments and dialogues with survivors reveal is what is frequently left out of witness statements. That is why, in part, women survivors are so often disbelieved and the charges against the perpetrators so often dismissed. The legal adversarial system reflects this in its attempts to discredit victims, to allude to past sexual behaviour, and to imply consent, ultimately discouraging legal action against alleged offenders.

DOMESTIC VIOLENCE AND RAPE CULTURE

In March 2015, the federal government declared that violence against women was a national crisis.[11] This in turn prompted national discussion of the scarcity of emergency services for women escaping violence, the impacts of financial abuse and coercive control, and social attitudes towards violence against women. The World Health Organization recently estimated that 35 per cent of women worldwide have experienced physical and/or sexual violence by a partner or a non-partner, such as a family member.[12] This violence is perpetrated against women and girls of all ages, ethnicities and social classes.

Violence against women has historical and cultural underpinnings and is maintained by social and systemic practices. All too often it is still regarded as inevitable, a view which implies the impossibility of change and reinforces contemporary gender inequality. The social and cultural constructions of gendered power and violence are central to any understanding of rape culture. We need to think about violence as a continuum that includes physical and non-physical forms of abuse.

'Rape culture' is a powerful statement about sexual violence and its embedded position in our society. To dismantle that culture, we need to consider the strategies of fear, threat, denial and confusion that undermine women's experiences. A rape culture is a complex system of values and practices built on the acceptability of sexual violence, and on how the individual and collective experiences of women are shaped in such a way as to trivialise the effects of trauma. And this refusal to acknowledge violence and to blame the victim is all too often supported by our medical and legal systems, which can leave women feeling isolated, disempowered, and with few options for support.

Women consistently describe experiencing high levels of emotional distress when they engage with hospitals and mental health services; they can feel overwhelmed, sometimes suicidal. Such reports have prompted conversations about the degree of understanding of gender-based violence in medical settings, and poorly coordinated emergency models of response that incorporate safety and mental health support. Within mental health services, there are also concerns about how well recognised are the impacts of gender violence, and the efficacy and availability of trauma-focused interventions and treatments. There are ongoing debates around the misuse of diagnoses that pathologise women and concentrate solely on their vulnerabilities and 'victimhood'. Some services perpetuate stereotypes of female masochism and reflexively use labels such as 'personality disorder' as an explanation of how and why some women feel trapped.

The next two cases involve women whose lives have been severely affected by long-term abuse, and who are determined to seek justice through the legal system. Their stories illustrate the difficult process of coming to terms with abuse, recognising it as a violent strategy to undermine a woman's sense of both reality and control. It is important to acknowledge such traumatic experiences if we are to assist these women to rebuild a sense of self-efficacy.

DEALING WITH SELF-BLAME: JOANNE

Joanne was a thirty-year-old woman working in the private financial industry who now lived with her mother after leaving a seven-year relationship. She was involved in police action against her former partner, who had been charged with breaching a violence order and with stalking and threatening behaviour. However, Joanne did not want to confide in friends or work colleagues, explaining that she felt a deep sense of shame that she had been involved in an abusive relationship, and that she feared she would be judged by others as 'a weak victim'. She did not believe that anyone would understand why she had stayed in this damaging relationship, why she had tried so hard to improve the interactions with her partner by adapting her behaviour to his demands and constantly trying to placate him—especially in light of how confused she herself was about her attempts to save the relationship, and how she had come to blame herself for the conflict.

I worked with Joanne for a year before she was able to start viewing her former partner as abusive. She eventually described him as volatile, with rapid shifts to anger and violence; she had feared for her life following an episode in which he choked her. He had repeatedly denigrated her, describing her as unattractive and stupid, telling her that she was lucky to have him as no-one else would put up with her behaviour. He even blamed her for his temper, saying that she had provoked him. When she tried to say that he was overreacting or being unreasonable, he would become enraged and call her 'insane'. He would deny abusive episodes, then destroy or hide her possessions, deliberately make a mess and then demand she clean it up, and throw away food she had made for him. Joanne became progressively more isolated and withdrawn, caught in a state of high anxiety. When she finally told her partner that she thought she should leave, he physically assaulted her and then threated to kill himself unless she apologised for hurting him. Joanne said she felt sorry for him, as he had come from a violent home where he'd been physically abused by his father—she saw it as her responsibility to help him recover.

Joanne said her own early family life was ruled by a frightening and domineering father and a quiet and harassed mother. She recalled her father being violent towards her mother when intoxicated, and being told by her mother that they should run away together and hide. She was so anxious at the age of six that she would check on her mother at night. Joanne had an older brother who was close to his father. When her father left the family when Joanne was ten years old, her brother became the dominant male in the household and verbally and emotionally abused Joanne and her mother. Joanne found it very painful to reflect on these early experiences and the ways in which they had shaped her expectations of male behaviour. She was angry with herself for enduring an adult relationship in which the abuse of her childhood was repeated, and for not realising the terrible situation she was in until she felt trapped.

Joanne said that, at first, her partner was charming and attentive, but this began to change after a few months. She then described the various ways in which her partner had systematically eroded her sense of agency and self-confidence until she could not trust her own judgement or sense of reality. Not surprisingly, she became chronically anxious and depressed, experienced episodes of panic and agitation, and had suicidal thoughts. She was prescribed an antidepressant by her local doctor, who was concerned about her level of risk and her mental health. But it was only after the attempted strangulation that Joanne realised that her partner 'hated her' and had destructive impulses. She fled when he was asleep—several months later, it occurred to her that if she had stayed in the relationship, she may well have died.

During our therapy, it was important for Joanne to be able to piece together an understanding of the relationship, how she had lost a sense of herself in the ongoing dynamic of trying to change herself while her partner seemed intent on destroying her sense of reality. The experience had left her with, among other things, an uncontrollable tremor, a frequent inability to sleep and ongoing panic attacks. She faced a long and hard path in resurrecting her self-esteem and self-efficacy. She would need to be listened to in a non-judgemental way and have some space to reflect on her former partner's patterns of, and responsibility for, psychological abuse. She also would need to reflect on the attempts she had made to survive such a disturbing environment and to contextualise her self-blame and shame.

It was important to help Joanne to see her mental health issues largely as symptoms of abuse, including being stalked by her ex-partner and threatened. She also needed to be assisted to understand his motivations and capacity for destructiveness, rather than repeatedly asking whether what had happened was 'really that bad'. Of course, as time went on, Joanne continued to grieve a relationship she had once hoped would be ongoing, but after twelve months of working with me, she could finally name her former partner as a perpetrator of domestic violence and acknowledge that she could not help him. Joanne's recovery continues.

TRYING TO BE VALUED: SARA

Sara was a 25-year-old woman, living on her own, who had previously worked in an administrative role for five years, during which time she had been in a relationship with a senior manager of her organisation. Sara told me that she initially had positive feelings about her manager's attentions, but that she began to feel uncomfortable when she became conscious that he was flirtatious and sexually suggestive. Like Joanne, Sara would see her relationship deteriorate after a period in which she was pleased to be favoured. Sara described herself as young and naive at that time, with little experience of relationships—and certainly not one with a man twenty years older than her.

Sara's family were members of a conservative religious group living in a regional area. She described her father as strict and controlling and her mother as submissive, although she denied any violence in her early life. Keen for new experiences after finishing school, and in the wake of ongoing conflict with her family, Sara made the difficult decision to leave home, whereupon she headed to the city for employment.

Sara had been made aware early on that the manager had a history of sexual behaviour with young staff, but she had not accepted this at the time. She did notice that he would become angry if she did not respond to some of his sexualised behaviours, and eventually she did not want to be left alone with him at work. On a few occasions, he grabbed and physically hurt her, leaving bruises. But she forgave him when he apologised and said he would not do this again. She started meeting him after work, drinking alcohol to ease her anxiety, and began to wish that the rendezvous might develop into an ongoing relationship.

Sara also described increasing efforts on her part to support her manager, who she saw as very stressed at work. He arranged for her to work more closely with him and continued to sexualise their interactions. She heard some comments from other staff and distanced herself from those colleagues, which only increased her isolation. She still had very mixed feelings about the manager but maintained a hope that he would come to really value her. However, there was little evidence that he did. He would get angry with her when he was anxious and blame her for any mistakes, telling her she was slow and stupid. He would say that he did not know why he kept her on and reminded her that if she was not a bit more 'friendly', he might terminate her employment. It was at an end-of-year function, when she was intoxicated, that Sara found herself being raped by her manager while semi-conscious. He drove her home, and the rape was never discussed. He then commenced a pattern of regular visits to her home when he was drunk, demanding sex, to which she did not consent.

Sara felt trapped, yet she wanted to protect her job. She was dependent on the manager and became anxious in her attempts to placate him. Over the next four years, he became angrier and denigrated her. He began to hit her, and he demanded sadomasochistic sex which she did not want. His behaviour towards her also deteriorated at work, where he treated her with contempt and publicly ridiculed her. Sara said she had little support from other staff members, who all seemed afraid of the manager. Feeling increasingly hopeless, she became depressed. She just did not understand why the relationship had taken this turn, why the manager would treat her this way.

A TRAUMA-FOCUSED APPROACH

For Sara and Joanne, a major focus of their treatment has been to support the development of a narrative which allows them to communicate the story of what happened and to dismantle the sense of shame and secrecy around the trauma. Sara finally was able to leave work, but only after a significant assault witnessed by others in the office. She now faces the difficulties of legal action and remains uncertain if this is worth pursuing, as it serves to keep her shackled to events she wishes she could forget. She is frightened that she will never trust anyone again and will remain isolated and alone—she has not even disclosed her experiences to her family, fearing rejection. Sara also struggles to understand the manager's motivation, anger and violent coercive behaviour. She feels she was trapped in the role of a 'sex slave' and has been left with a view of herself as damaged, spoiled.

Both Joanne and Sara suffered long-term abuse and violence. Both lived in a state of confusion and frozen anxiety. Such responses to an ordeal protect the individual and serve as a necessary defence in some situations. The price, however, is significant, including numbness, and experiencing memories in disturbing dreams and flashbacks that prompt doubts in the women about their recollections and their sanity.

A trauma-focused approach is vital for survivors of domestic abuse to develop a firmer sense of identity, a stronger sense of self, and a language in which the trauma can be expressed. Weak, passive and frightened women serve the interests of rape culture. But all the research show us that if we focus on the reality of abuse, if we help women to find a way to articulate what has happened, they are able to begin the painful, hard work of regaining their mental health.

WOMEN, FEMINISM AND
THE POLITICAL CHALLENGE

If the rape culture we live in is to be changed, we need to rethink our mental health services and most particularly our therapeutic approaches. The feminist psychotherapists of the 1970s focused on a sociological understanding of gender and power. The Me Too movement of the early twenty-first century, along with parallel revelations that misogyny is not just alive and well but thriving in modern society, has posed a new challenge to those of us involved in supporting traumatised women. Contemporary theory recognises that sexuality is a continuum, that sex, gender and desire aren't immutable givens. The complexity of human nature doesn't lend itself to simplistic solutions. It shouldn't make clinicians reach reflexively for the prescription pad or candles or mindfulness seminars.

This isn't just a matter of theoretical interest, because many of these issues demand urgent attention and care. When I see Ophelia or Elizabeth or Jane's distress, I know I must respond. These woman are clamouring to be heard, to be able to speak and to define themselves. There is a struggle between a desire for dependency and moving towards autonomy and self-actualisation. The latter notions have of course been criticised as narcissistic, overly individualistic, insufficiently focused on the importance of connectedness and nurturing relationships. This may be the tension the psychoanalyst Jacques Lacan scathingly described as 'the psychology of free enterprise'. But for survivors, the task of reclaiming selfhood, a feeling of agency, precedes any work regarding feeling connected to others.

As the stories in this book show, women's experiences of abuse and violence can have long-term impacts on their mental health and emotional wellbeing. For women abused in childhood, typically within families, there may be disruptions to the development of a sense of identity and autonomy and to the formation of relationships, and ongoing difficulty in managing emotions. Our collective avoidance of the reality of child abuse and exploitation has resulted in devastating effects in survivors who feel abandoned, invalidated and chronically traumatised. Lives are derailed by early abuse. Similarly, the impacts of gender-based violence in adults may undermine self-identity, safety and the capacity to deal with trauma symptoms.

Complex trauma-related issues often require complex and coordinated interventions and supports. Following on from the immediate needs of safety, health and legal concerns, it is crucial to help women understand the nature of assault and violence. Specialist interventions work to improve the processing of trauma symptoms, stress management and the development of a sense of personal control. We need to ensure the integration of trauma models of care with mental health approaches, so that we can offer more to survivors than information and cognitive approaches. These practices go beyond simple disclosure to providing therapeutic relationships where a survivor can rebuild a sense of validation and trust. There is currently very limited access to this level of support, which all too often leaves traumatised survivors seeking ineffective or even harmful help.

The current moment is one of deep confrontation with misogyny. The stakes are high, and there can be a significant backlash—the price of speaking out is felt at both the personal and social levels. There is a confusing complexity about group and personal identities and how they intersect. For example, the oppression of women of colour has a specific history and is grounded in specific experiences; the same applies to gender-diverse and trans women. The recent focus on gendered violence and toxic masculinity has prompted outrage from right-wing media commentators, who reach for their limited vocabulary and 'feminism as man hating' rhetoric. But preventing violence to women will not be possible without a focus on our fundamental rights to diversity, self-determination, safety and respect. The current political response to the 'sexual abuse crisis' and the 'woman problem' is an attempt to manage these issues with as little significant change as possible. Hence, we are surrounded by multiple committees of inquiry, legal arguments and obfuscation, with glib references to principles. Meanwhile, little is said about eliminating misogyny and oppression.

It is hard to understand the motivations underlying male violence and sexual assault without understanding the historical framework and the nature of coercive control and the exercise of power. In women, this induces silence, blocks dissent, and creates self-doubt, shame and loathing. There are many ways of thinking about paralysis in the face of trauma and abuse, but it is always gendered. Not only are women seen as weak and hysterical, they are also to blame for inviting their own abuse and should therefore feel shame and remain silent.

Theory is one thing, but we must examine the reality of male violence and men's need to control femininity, as well as the ways in which this translates into acts of hatred, revenge and murder. Children are used in these battles, where the greatest injury to the mother is to kill her children, relegating her to a life of grief and pain. What is remarkable about this is the fact that the regular murder of women and children, and widespread sexual assault and violence, do not result in ongoing mass protests and calls for change.

Sustaining protest, maintaining the rage, is of course difficult in the face of invalidating treatment and complacency. While for some it is too painful to acknowledge this reality, for others, this undercurrent of violence towards women has become normalised. This is the essence of rape culture. So how do we resist the assumption that this is all natural, inevitable, and therefore acceptable?

Change is necessarily complex and goes beyond the confines of party politics. It begins with the imaginative exercise of committing to the vision of a society free from sexism and gender-based violence. We need to develop a language for what does not currently exist, a language of possibility that contributes to a different representation of sex and gender. This language is an aspirational tool for dismantling the systems, institutions and beliefs that maintain the status quo. Admittedly, this level of change starts largely in the perennially vilified humanities, which admit and welcome humanity's incredible diversity. This is where the foundations of rape culture and oppression can be de-legitimated.

The processes of change operate at systemic and institutional levels, within political discourse, and within individual and group psychology. Much of the recent response to the crisis of sexual abuse has concentrated on attempts to tighten the operations of institutions to address issues such as workplace discrimination, complaints processes and legal systems. These efforts are needed and necessary, but it remains unclear if they contribute to any significant shifts in assumptions about misogyny. As its political reaction to disclosures of abuse, the current Australian Government has worked to strengthen systemic responses, investigate approaches to safety and how complaints are made, and promote 'empathy' as a therapeutic approach. And yet, ironically, there is a clear concurrent process of blocking any independent external review of incidents, and a retreat to 'rule of law' arguments to limit accountability and invalidate victims.

~

The protest movement we have witnessed in 2021 has challenged the ubiquitous 'contain and control' political tactics and the silencing of survivor testimony. The disclosure of the extent of violence and misogyny in our society, and the analysis of patriarchy and rape culture, have long formed part of the feminist agenda. We are now all privy to public and frank accounts of this reality—they are painful to tell and to hear. But calls for social justice and accountability largely have not been met with effective action. An initial powerful process of disclosure from Me Too raised awareness of the extent of the problem. The next stage became known as What Next?, a reference to the great capacity of social systems to enter a state of minimal action and wait until the storm passes, making a few desultory concessions only when absolutely necessary. Historically, this has been an effective strategy to curtail social dissent. Small changes have come at a high price.

This discussion has highlighted the price paid by those who disclose abuse or challenge systems that deny a voice to survivors and act to perpetuate repression. The priority now should be to provide services for women with limited access to specialised care and support. The need for expertise in working with abuse and trauma is acute, particularly at a time when there are increasing rates of disclosure and attempts to access support. This has been evidenced by the significant increases in calls to domestic violence support numbers during the pandemic lockdowns in Australia, when relationship stress and conflict have escalated.

The What Next? question remains. Those of us working directly with victim-survivors and their children see far too much of the potentially devastating and long-term consequences of rape culture. Ironically, while we see the need for appropriate understanding and therapeutic interventions, we also see a clear need to contextualise women's suffering and to investigate the systemic underpinnings of abuse. Abuse does not occur at random, or in a vacuum. It emerges in the context of deeply held but erroneous assumptions around gender, the position of women in the community, and the inevitability of male power. We need to resist the drive to pathologise women's experiences using a language of essential biological inferiority and a tendency to mental disorder.

We need gender-specific models of care and treatment for the enormous range of mental disorders and psychological issues stemming from rape culture, ones that can work with survivors' distress in a safe and informed way. We need to put women's voices and narratives at the centre of treatment systems, and to find new ways of listening to them.

ACKNOWLEDGEMENTS

Some of the ideas in this book have had a long gestation, much like the systems of power and gender that are discussed. I am fortunate to have had time and exposure to a variety of approaches for thinking about these issues, and to have encountered women scholars and clinicians who have contributed a huge amount to the development of feminism and psychoanalysis in Australia and internationally.

Back in the 1970s, I was able to immerse myself in the then radically new interpretations of Freud and new ways of thinking about the construction of femininity. The French feminist psychoanalysts and their re-reading of Lacan were taught—in a way that shaped all of my future work—by Elizabeth

Grosz in the Department of General Philosophy at the University of Sydney. I studied Psychology at a time when there was a psychoanalyst in the department—an endangered species in academic psychology—namely John Maze, and I listened to interpretations of Virginia Woolf's *To the Lighthouse*. Of course, at the time I had little idea of the significance of these influences.

Later, in medicine and psychiatry, I became painfully aware of the real impact of battling patriarchal norms and gendered power, and I remain grateful to the women of power in academia and government I worked with. My thanks go to Professor Beverley Raphael (now deceased) and Professor Carolyn Quadrio, who was, and remains, courageous and outspoken, and who led a movement of women in psychiatry. I can only attempt to offer this sort of mentorship and support.

Lastly, I thank my mother, who paved her own way and taught me the importance of carving out a space in which to think and be creative, and to guard it to the end.

NOTES

1   Federal Court of Australia, 'BLUE Card 1: Jo Dyer Transcript', posted June 2021, https://www.fedcourt. gov.au/services/access-to-files-and-transcripts/ online-files/dyer-v-chrysanthou/2021_05_25-Exhibit-5-redacted.pdf (viewed July 2021).

2   Royal Commission into Institutional Responses to Child Sexual Abuse, 'Final Report', Commonwealth of Australia, 2017, https://www.childabuseroyal commission.gov.au/final-report (viewed July 2021).

3   Pseudonyms have been used and de-identification has taken place in all of these stories.

4   Tom Stayner, 'Critics and Political Opponents Have Raised Concerns that Senator Stoker Is Unsuitable for Her Role Because of Her Positions on Transgender Issues and Abortion', SBS News, 30 March 2021, https://www.sbs.com.au/news/critics-concerned-by-amanda-stoker-s-derogatory-views-on-transgender-issues-as-she-moves-into-women-s-portfolio (viewed July 2021).

5   Simone de Beauvoir, *The Second Sex*, Gallimard, Paris, 1949.

6   Juliet Mitchell, *Mad Men and Medusas: Reclaiming Hysteria*, Basic Books, New York, 2000.

7   Roxane Gay, *Hunger: A Memoir of (My) Body*, HarperCollins, New York, 2017.

8   Jacey Fortin, 'Roxane Gay Promotes New Book and Calls out Podcast for "Fat-Phobia"', *The New York Times*, 13 June 2017, https://www.nytimes.com/2017/06/13/books/mamamia-roxane-gay-mia-freedman.html (viewed July 2021).

9   Julia Kristeva, *Powers of Horror: An Essay on Abjection*, Columbia University Press, New York, 1982.

10 Sigmund Freud, *Dora: An Analysis of a Case of Hysteria*, Touchstone Books, New York, 1997.

11 Tony Abbott and Michaelia Cash, 'National Awareness Campaign to Reduce Violence against Women and Children', press release, Prime Minister of Australia, 4 March 2015.

12 World Health Organization, 'Violence against Women', fact sheet, 9 March 2021, https://www.who.int/en/news-room/fact-sheets/detail/violence-against-women (viewed July 2021).

IN THE NATIONAL INTEREST

Other books on the issues that matter: